This Food Journal Belongs To:

_____

My Food Journal   Date:_____

Today My Healthy Choices Were:

Breakfast:_____
_____

Lunch:_____
_____

Dinner:_____
_____

Today I Drank _ Glasses Of Water

I Tried These New Foods Today:
_____
_____

My Food Group Scale:

Grains	Fruits	Dairy	Protein	Veggies

My Food Journal   Date:_____

Today My Healthy Choices Were:

Breakfast:_____
_____

Lunch:_____
_____

Dinner:_____
_____

Today I Drank _ Glasses Of Water

I Tried These New Foods Today:
_____
_____

My Food Group Scale:

Grains   Fruits   Dairy   Protein   Veggies

My Food Journal   Date:_____

Today My Healthy Choices Were:

Breakfast:_____
_____

Lunch:_____
_____

Dinner:_____
_____

Today I Drank _ Glasses Of Water

I Tried These New Foods Today:
_____
_____

My Food Group Scale:

Grains	Fruits	Dairy	Protein	Veggies

My Food Journal   Date:_____

Today My Healthy Choices Were:

Breakfast:_____
_____

Lunch:_____
_____

Dinner:_____
_____

Today I Drank _ Glasses Of Water

I Tried These New Foods Today:
_____
_____

My Food Group Scale:

Grains	Fruits	Dairy	Protein	Veggies

My Food Journal   Date:_____

Today My Healthy Choices Were:

Breakfast:_____
_____

Lunch:_____
_____

Dinner:_____
_____

Today I Drank _ Glasses Of Water

I Tried These New Foods Today:
_____
_____

My Food Group Scale:

Grains	Fruits	Dairy	Protein	Veggies

My Food Journal   Date:_____

Today My Healthy Choices Were:

Breakfast:_____
_____

Lunch:_____
_____

Dinner:_____
_____

Today I Drank _ Glasses Of Water

I Tried These New Foods Today:
_____
_____

My Food Group Scale:

Grains	Fruits	Dairy	Protein	Veggies

My Food Journal   Date:_____

Today My Healthy Choices Were:

Breakfast:_____
_____

Lunch:_____
_____

Dinner:_____
_____

Today I Drank _ Glasses Of Water

I Tried These New Foods Today:
_____
_____

My Food Group Scale:

Grains	Fruits	Dairy	Protein	Veggies

My Food Journal   Date:_____

Today My Healthy Choices Were:

Breakfast:_____
_____

Lunch:_____
_____

Dinner:_____
_____

Today I Drank _ Glasses Of Water

I Tried These New Foods Today:
_____
_____

My Food Group Scale:

Grains   Fruits   Dairy   Protein   Veggies
 ☆   ☆   ☆   ☆   ☆

My Food Journal

Date:_____

Today My Healthy Choices Were:

Breakfast:_____
_____

Lunch:_____
_____

Dinner:_____
_____

Today I Drank _ Glasses Of Water

I Tried These New Foods Today:
_____
_____

My Food Group Scale:

Grains	Fruits	Dairy	Protein	Veggies

My Food Journal   Date:_____

Today My Healthy Choices Were:

Breakfast:_____
_____

Lunch:_____
_____

Dinner:_____
_____

Today I Drank _ Glasses Of Water

I Tried These New Foods Today:
_____
_____

My Food Group Scale:

Grains	Fruits	Dairy	Protein	Veggies

My Food Journal   Date:_____

Today My Healthy Choices Were:

Breakfast:_____
_____

Lunch:_____
_____

Dinner:_____
_____

Today I Drank _ Glasses Of Water

I Tried These New Foods Today:
_____
_____

My Food Group Scale:

Grains	Fruits	Dairy	Protein	Veggies

My Food Journal   Date:_____

Today My Healthy Choices Were:

Breakfast:_____
_____

Lunch:_____
_____

Dinner:_____
_____

Today I Drank _ Glasses Of Water

I Tried These New Foods Today:
_____
_____

My Food Group Scale:

Grains	Fruits	Dairy	Protein	Veggies

My Food Journal   Date:_____

Today My Healthy Choices Were:

Breakfast:_____
_____

Lunch:_____
_____

Dinner:_____
_____

Today I Drank _ Glasses Of Water

I Tried These New Foods Today:
_____
_____

My Food Group Scale:

Grains   Fruits   Dairy   Protein   Veggies

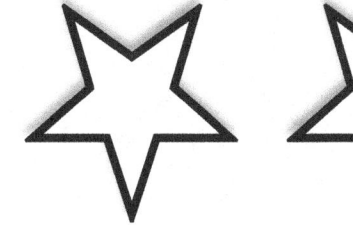    

My Food Journal   Date:_____

Today My Healthy Choices Were:

Breakfast:_____
_____

Lunch:_____
_____

Dinner:_____
_____

Today I Drank _ Glasses Of Water

I Tried These New Foods Today:
_____
_____

My Food Group Scale:

Grains   Fruits   Dairy   Protein   Veggies

My Food Journal   Date:_____

Today My Healthy Choices Were:

Breakfast:_____
_____

Lunch:_____
_____

Dinner:_____
_____

Today I Drank _ Glasses Of Water

I Tried These New Foods Today:
_____
_____

My Food Group Scale:

Grains	Fruits	Dairy	Protein	Veggies

My Food Journal   Date:_____

Today My Healthy Choices Were:

Breakfast:_____
_____

Lunch:_____
_____

Dinner:_____
_____

Today I Drank _ Glasses Of Water

I Tried These New Foods Today:
_____
_____

My Food Group Scale:

Grains	Fruits	Dairy	Protein	Veggies

My Food Journal   Date:_____

Today My Healthy Choices Were:

Breakfast:_____
_____

Lunch:_____
_____

Dinner:_____
_____

Today I Drank _ Glasses Of Water

I Tried These New Foods Today:
_____
_____

My Food Group Scale:

Grains	Fruits	Dairy	Protein	Veggies

My Food Journal   Date:_____

Today My Healthy Choices Were:

Breakfast:_____
_____

Lunch:_____
_____

Dinner:_____
_____

Today I Drank _ Glasses Of Water

I Tried These New Foods Today:
_____
_____

My Food Group Scale:

Grains   Fruits   Dairy   Protein   Veggies

My Food Journal

Date:_____

Today My Healthy Choices Were:

Breakfast:_____
_____

Lunch:_____
_____

Dinner:_____
_____

Today I Drank _ Glasses Of Water

I Tried These New Foods Today:
_____
_____

My Food Group Scale:

Grains	Fruits	Dairy	Protein	Veggies

My Food Journal   Date:_____

Today My Healthy Choices Were:

Breakfast:_____
_____

Lunch:_____
_____

Dinner:_____
_____

Today I Drank _ Glasses Of Water

I Tried These New Foods Today:
_____
_____

My Food Group Scale:

Grains	Fruits	Dairy	Protein	Veggies

My Food Journal   Date:_____

Today My Healthy Choices Were:

Breakfast:_____
_____

Lunch:_____
_____

Dinner:_____
_____

Today I Drank _ Glasses Of Water

I Tried These New Foods Today:
_____
_____

My Food Group Scale:

Grains	Fruits	Dairy	Protein	Veggies

My Food Journal   Date:_____

Today My Healthy Choices Were:

Breakfast:_____
_____

Lunch:_____
_____

Dinner:_____
_____

Today I Drank _ Glasses Of Water

I Tried These New Foods Today:
_____
_____

My Food Group Scale:

Grains	Fruits	Dairy	Protein	Veggies

My Food Journal   Date:_____

Today My Healthy Choices Were:

Breakfast:_____
_____

Lunch:_____
_____

Dinner:_____
_____

Today I Drank _ Glasses Of Water

I Tried These New Foods Today:
_____
_____

My Food Group Scale:

Grains	Fruits	Dairy	Protein	Veggies

My Food Journal   Date:_____

Today My Healthy Choices Were:

Breakfast:_____
_____

Lunch:_____
_____

Dinner:_____
_____

Today I Drank _ Glasses Of Water

I Tried These New Foods Today:
_____
_____

My Food Group Scale:

Grains	Fruits	Dairy	Protein	Veggies

My Food Journal   Date:_____

Today My Healthy Choices Were:

Breakfast:_____
_____

Lunch:_____
_____

Dinner:_____
_____

Today I Drank _ Glasses Of Water

I Tried These New Foods Today:
_____
_____

My Food Group Scale:

Grains	Fruits	Dairy	Protein	Veggies

My Food Journal   Date:_____

Today My Healthy Choices Were:

Breakfast:_____
_____

Lunch:_____
_____

Dinner:_____
_____

Today I Drank _ Glasses Of Water

I Tried These New Foods Today:
_____
_____

My Food Group Scale:

Grains   Fruits   Dairy   Protein   Veggies

My Food Journal   Date:_____

Today My Healthy Choices Were:

Breakfast:_____
_____

Lunch:_____
_____

Dinner:_____
_____

Today I Drank _ Glasses Of Water

I Tried These New Foods Today:
_____
_____

My Food Group Scale:

Grains	Fruits	Dairy	Protein	Veggies

My Food Journal   Date:_____

Today My Healthy Choices Were:

Breakfast:_____
_____

Lunch:_____
_____

Dinner:_____
_____

Today I Drank _ Glasses Of Water

I Tried These New Foods Today:
_____
_____

My Food Group Scale:

Grains   Fruits   Dairy   Protein   Veggies

My Food Journal   Date:_____

Today My Healthy Choices Were:

Breakfast:_____
_____

Lunch:_____
_____

Dinner:_____
_____

Today I Drank _ Glasses Of Water

I Tried These New Foods Today:
_____
_____

My Food Group Scale:

Grains   Fruits   Dairy   Protein   Veggies

My Food Journal   Date:_____

Today My Healthy Choices Were:

Breakfast:_____
_____

Lunch:_____
_____

Dinner:_____
_____

Today I Drank _ Glasses Of Water

I Tried These New Foods Today:
_____
_____

My Food Group Scale:

Grains	Fruits	Dairy	Protein	Veggies

My Food Journal   Date:_____

Today My Healthy Choices Were:

Breakfast:_____
_____

Lunch:_____
_____

Dinner:_____
_____

Today I Drank _ Glasses Of Water

I Tried These New Foods Today:
_____
_____

My Food Group Scale:

Grains	Fruits	Dairy	Protein	Veggies

My Food Journal   Date:_____

Today My Healthy Choices Were:

Breakfast:_____
_____

Lunch:_____
_____

Dinner:_____
_____

Today I Drank _ Glasses Of Water

I Tried These New Foods Today:
_____
_____

My Food Group Scale:

Grains	Fruits	Dairy	Protein	Veggies

My Food Journal   Date:_____

Today My Healthy Choices Were:

Breakfast:_____
_____

Lunch:_____
_____

Dinner:_____
_____

Today I Drank _ Glasses Of Water

I Tried These New Foods Today:
_____
_____

My Food Group Scale:

Grains	Fruits	Dairy	Protein	Veggies

My Food Journal   Date:_____

Today My Healthy Choices Were:

Breakfast:_____
_____

Lunch:_____
_____

Dinner:_____
_____

Today I Drank _ Glasses Of Water

I Tried These New Foods Today:
_____
_____

My Food Group Scale:

Grains   Fruits   Dairy   Protein   Veggies

My Food Journal   Date:_____

Today My Healthy Choices Were:

Breakfast:_____
_____

Lunch:_____
_____

Dinner:_____
_____

Today I Drank _ Glasses Of Water

I Tried These New Foods Today:
_____
_____

My Food Group Scale:

Grains	Fruits	Dairy	Protein	Veggies

My Food Journal   Date:_____

Today My Healthy Choices Were:

Breakfast:_____
_____

Lunch:_____
_____

Dinner:_____
_____

Today I Drank _ Glasses Of Water

I Tried These New Foods Today:
_____
_____

My Food Group Scale:

Grains	Fruits	Dairy	Protein	Veggies

My Food Journal   Date:_____

Today My Healthy Choices Were:

Breakfast:_____
_____

Lunch:_____
_____

Dinner:_____
_____

Today I Drank _ Glasses Of Water

I Tried These New Foods Today:
_____
_____

My Food Group Scale:

Grains	Fruits	Dairy	Protein	Veggies

My Food Journal   Date:_____

Today My Healthy Choices Were:

Breakfast:_____
_____

Lunch:_____
_____

Dinner:_____
_____

Today I Drank _ Glasses Of Water

I Tried These New Foods Today:
_____
_____

My Food Group Scale:

Grains	Fruits	Dairy	Protein	Veggies

My Food Journal   Date:_____

Today My Healthy Choices Were:

Breakfast:_____
_____

Lunch:_____
_____

Dinner:_____
_____

Today I Drank _ Glasses Of Water

I Tried These New Foods Today:
_____
_____

My Food Group Scale:

Grains	Fruits	Dairy	Protein	Veggies

My Food Journal   Date:____

Today My Healthy Choices Were:

Breakfast:_____
_____

Lunch:_____
_____

Dinner:_____
_____

Today I Drank _ Glasses Of Water

I Tried These New Foods Today:
_____
_____

My Food Group Scale:

Grains	Fruits	Dairy	Protein	Veggies

My Food Journal   Date:_____

Today My Healthy Choices Were:

Breakfast:_____
_____

Lunch:_____
_____

Dinner:_____
_____

Today I Drank _ Glasses Of Water

I Tried These New Foods Today:
_____
_____

My Food Group Scale:

Grains   Fruits   Dairy   Protein   Veggies

My Food Journal   Date:_____

Today My Healthy Choices Were:

Breakfast:_____
_____

Lunch:_____
_____

Dinner:_____
_____

Today I Drank _ Glasses Of Water

I Tried These New Foods Today:
_____
_____

My Food Group Scale:

My Food Journal   Date:_____

Today My Healthy Choices Were:

Breakfast:_____
_____

Lunch:_____
_____

Dinner:_____
_____

Today I Drank _ Glasses Of Water

I Tried These New Foods Today:
_____
_____

My Food Group Scale:

| Grains | Fruits | Dairy | Protein | Veggies |

My Food Journal   Date:_____

Today My Healthy Choices Were:

Breakfast:_____
_____

Lunch:_____
_____

Dinner:_____
_____

Today I Drank _ Glasses Of Water

I Tried These New Foods Today:
_____
_____

My Food Group Scale:

Grains	Fruits	Dairy	Protein	Veggies

My Food Journal   Date:_____

Today My Healthy Choices Were:

Breakfast:_____
_____

Lunch:_____
_____

Dinner:_____
_____

Today I Drank _ Glasses Of Water

I Tried These New Foods Today:
_____
_____

My Food Group Scale:

Grains	Fruits	Dairy	Protein	Veggies

My Food Journal   Date:_____

Today My Healthy Choices Were:

Breakfast:_____
_____

Lunch:_____
_____

Dinner:_____
_____

Today I Drank _ Glasses Of Water

I Tried These New Foods Today:
_____
_____

My Food Group Scale:

Grains	Fruits	Dairy	Protein	Veggies

My Food Journal   Date:_____

Today My Healthy Choices Were:

Breakfast:_____
_____

Lunch:_____
_____

Dinner:_____
_____

Today I Drank _ Glasses Of Water

I Tried These New Foods Today:
_____
_____

My Food Group Scale:

Grains	Fruits	Dairy	Protein	Veggies

My Food Journal   Date:_____

Today My Healthy Choices Were:

Breakfast:_____
_____

Lunch:_____
_____

Dinner:_____
_____

Today I Drank _ Glasses Of Water

I Tried These New Foods Today:
_____
_____

My Food Group Scale:

Grains	Fruits	Dairy	Protein	Veggies

My Food Journal   Date:_____

Today My Healthy Choices Were:

Breakfast:_____
_____

Lunch:_____
_____

Dinner:_____
_____

Today I Drank _ Glasses Of Water

I Tried These New Foods Today:
_____
_____

My Food Group Scale:

| Grains | Fruits | Dairy | Protein | Veggies |

My Food Journal   Date:_____

Today My Healthy Choices Were:

Breakfast:_____
_____

Lunch:_____
_____

Dinner:_____
_____

Today I Drank _ Glasses Of Water

I Tried These New Foods Today:
_____
_____

My Food Group Scale:

Grains	Fruits	Dairy	Protein	Veggies

My Food Journal   Date:_____

Today My Healthy Choices Were:

Breakfast:_____
_____

Lunch:_____
_____

Dinner:_____
_____

Today I Drank _ Glasses Of Water

I Tried These New Foods Today:
_____
_____

My Food Group Scale:

Grains	Fruits	Dairy	Protein	Veggies

My Food Journal   Date:_____

Today My Healthy Choices Were:

Breakfast:_____
_____

Lunch:_____
_____

Dinner:_____
_____

Today I Drank _ Glasses Of Water

I Tried These New Foods Today:
_____
_____

My Food Group Scale:

Grains	Fruits	Dairy	Protein	Veggies

My Food Journal   Date:_____

Today My Healthy Choices Were:

Breakfast:_____
_____

Lunch:_____
_____

Dinner:_____
_____

Today I Drank _ Glasses Of Water

I Tried These New Foods Today:
_____
_____

My Food Group Scale:

Grains	Fruits	Dairy	Protein	Veggies

My Food Journal   Date:_____

Today My Healthy Choices Were:

Breakfast:_____
_____

Lunch:_____
_____

Dinner:_____
_____

Today I Drank _ Glasses Of Water

I Tried These New Foods Today:
_____
_____

My Food Group Scale:

Grains	Fruits	Dairy	Protein	Veggies

My Food Journal   Date:_____

Today My Healthy Choices Were:

Breakfast:_____
_____

Lunch:_____
_____

Dinner:_____
_____

Today I Drank _ Glasses Of Water

I Tried These New Foods Today:
_____
_____

My Food Group Scale:

Grains	Fruits	Dairy	Protein	Veggies

My Food Journal   Date:_____

Today My Healthy Choices Were:

Breakfast:_____
_____

Lunch:_____
_____

Dinner:_____
_____

Today I Drank _ Glasses Of Water

I Tried These New Foods Today:
_____
_____

My Food Group Scale:

Grains	Fruits	Dairy	Protein	Veggies

My Food Journal   Date:_____

Today My Healthy Choices Were:

Breakfast:_____
_____

Lunch:_____
_____

Dinner:_____
_____

Today I Drank _ Glasses Of Water

I Tried These New Foods Today:
_____
_____

My Food Group Scale:

Grains   Fruits   Dairy   Protein   Veggies

My Food Journal   Date:_____

Today My Healthy Choices Were:

Breakfast:_____
_____

Lunch:_____
_____

Dinner:_____
_____

Today I Drank _ Glasses Of Water

I Tried These New Foods Today:
_____
_____

My Food Group Scale:

Grains	Fruits	Dairy	Protein	Veggies

My Food Journal   Date:_____

Today My Healthy Choices Were:

Breakfast:_____
_____

Lunch:_____
_____

Dinner:_____
_____

Today I Drank _ Glasses Of Water

I Tried These New Foods Today:
_____
_____

My Food Group Scale:

Grains	Fruits	Dairy	Protein	Veggies

My Food Journal   Date:_____

Today My Healthy Choices Were:

Breakfast:_____
_____

Lunch:_____
_____

Dinner:_____
_____

Today I Drank _ Glasses Of Water

I Tried These New Foods Today:
_____
_____

My Food Group Scale:

Grains	Fruits	Dairy	Protein	Veggies

My Food Journal   Date:_____

Today My Healthy Choices Were:

Breakfast:_____
_____

Lunch:_____
_____

Dinner:_____
_____

Today I Drank _ Glasses Of Water

I Tried These New Foods Today:
_____
_____

My Food Group Scale:

Grains	Fruits	Dairy	Protein	Veggies

My Food Journal   Date:_____

Today My Healthy Choices Were:

Breakfast:_____
_____

Lunch:_____
_____

Dinner:_____
_____

Today I Drank _ Glasses Of Water

I Tried These New Foods Today:
_____
_____

My Food Group Scale:

Grains	Fruits	Dairy	Protein	Veggies
☆	☆	☆	☆	☆

My Food Journal   Date:_____

Today My Healthy Choices Were:

Breakfast:_____
_____

Lunch:_____
_____

Dinner:_____
_____

Today I Drank _ Glasses Of Water

I Tried These New Foods Today:
_____
_____

My Food Group Scale:

Grains	Fruits	Dairy	Protein	Veggies

My Food Journal   Date:_____

Today My Healthy Choices Were:

Breakfast:_____
_____

Lunch:_____
_____

Dinner:_____
_____

Today I Drank _ Glasses Of Water

I Tried These New Foods Today:
_____
_____

My Food Group Scale:

Grains	Fruits	Dairy	Protein	Veggies

My Food Journal   Date:_____

Today My Healthy Choices Were:

Breakfast:_____
_____

Lunch:_____
_____

Dinner:_____
_____

Today I Drank _ Glasses Of Water

I Tried These New Foods Today:
_____
_____

My Food Group Scale:

Grains	Fruits	Dairy	Protein	Veggies

My Food Journal   Date:_____

Today My Healthy Choices Were:

Breakfast:_____
_____

Lunch:_____
_____

Dinner:_____
_____

Today I Drank _ Glasses Of Water

I Tried These New Foods Today:
_____
_____

My Food Group Scale:

Grains	Fruits	Dairy	Protein	Veggies

My Food Journal   Date:_____

Today My Healthy Choices Were:

Breakfast:_____
_____

Lunch:_____
_____

Dinner:_____
_____

Today I Drank _ Glasses Of Water

I Tried These New Foods Today:
_____
_____

My Food Group Scale:

Grains   Fruits   Dairy   Protein   Veggies

☆   ☆   ☆   ☆   ☆

My Food Journal   Date:_____

Today My Healthy Choices Were:

Breakfast:_____
_____

Lunch:_____
_____

Dinner:_____
_____

Today I Drank _ Glasses Of Water

I Tried These New Foods Today:
_____
_____

My Food Group Scale:

Grains   Fruits   Dairy   Protein   Veggies

My Food Journal

Date:_____

Today My Healthy Choices Were:

Breakfast:_____
_____

Lunch:_____
_____

Dinner:_____
_____

Today I Drank _ Glasses Of Water

I Tried These New Foods Today:
_____
_____

My Food Group Scale:

Grains	Fruits	Dairy	Protein	Veggies

My Food Journal   Date:_____

Today My Healthy Choices Were:

Breakfast:_____
_____

Lunch:_____
_____

Dinner:_____
_____

Today I Drank _ Glasses Of Water

I Tried These New Foods Today:
_____
_____

My Food Group Scale:

Grains   Fruits   Dairy   Protein   Veggies

My Food Journal   Date:_____

Today My Healthy Choices Were:

Breakfast:_____
_____

Lunch:_____
_____

Dinner:_____
_____

Today I Drank _ Glasses Of Water

I Tried These New Foods Today:
_____
_____

My Food Group Scale:

Grains   Fruits   Dairy   Protein   Veggies

My Food Journal   Date:_____

Today My Healthy Choices Were:

Breakfast:_____
_____

Lunch:_____
_____

Dinner:_____
_____

Today I Drank _ Glasses Of Water

I Tried These New Foods Today:
_____
_____

My Food Group Scale:

Grains	Fruits	Dairy	Protein	Veggies

My Food Journal   Date:____

Today My Healthy Choices Were:

Breakfast:_____
_____

Lunch:_____
_____

Dinner:_____
_____

Today I Drank _ Glasses Of Water

I Tried These New Foods Today:
_____
_____

My Food Group Scale:

Grains	Fruits	Dairy	Protein	Veggies

My Food Journal   Date:_____

Today My Healthy Choices Were:

Breakfast:_____
_____

Lunch:_____
_____

Dinner:_____
_____

Today I Drank _ Glasses Of Water

I Tried These New Foods Today:
_____
_____

My Food Group Scale:

Grains	Fruits	Dairy	Protein	Veggies

My Food Journal   Date:_____

Today My Healthy Choices Were:

Breakfast:_____
_____

Lunch:_____
_____

Dinner:_____
_____

Today I Drank _ Glasses Of Water

I Tried These New Foods Today:
_____
_____

My Food Group Scale:

Grains	Fruits	Dairy	Protein	Veggies

My Food Journal

Date:_____

Today My Healthy Choices Were:

Breakfast:_____
_____

Lunch:_____
_____

Dinner:_____
_____

Today I Drank _ Glasses Of Water

I Tried These New Foods Today:
_____
_____

My Food Group Scale:

Grains	Fruits	Dairy	Protein	Veggies
☆	☆	☆	☆	☆

My Food Journal   Date:_____

Today My Healthy Choices Were:

Breakfast:_____
_____

Lunch:_____
_____

Dinner:_____
_____

Today I Drank _ Glasses Of Water

I Tried These New Foods Today:
_____
_____

My Food Group Scale:

Grains	Fruits	Dairy	Protein	Veggies

My Food Journal   Date:_____

Today My Healthy Choices Were:

Breakfast:_____
_____

Lunch:_____
_____

Dinner:_____
_____

Today I Drank _ Glasses Of Water

I Tried These New Foods Today:
_____
_____

My Food Group Scale:

Grains	Fruits	Dairy	Protein	Veggies

My Food Journal   Date:_____

Today My Healthy Choices Were:

Breakfast:_____
_____

Lunch:_____
_____

Dinner:_____
_____

Today I Drank _ Glasses Of Water

I Tried These New Foods Today:
_____
_____

My Food Group Scale:

Grains	Fruits	Dairy	Protein	Veggies

My Food Journal   Date:_____

Today My Healthy Choices Were:

Breakfast:_____
_____

Lunch:_____
_____

Dinner:_____
_____

Today I Drank _ Glasses Of Water

I Tried These New Foods Today:
_____
_____

My Food Group Scale:

Grains	Fruits	Dairy	Protein	Veggies

Made in the USA
Middletown, DE
03 March 2023

26088735R00046